Mami, what is Immigration?

Anissa Pérez

Illustrated by Nicol Belvedere

© 2025 Anissa Pérez
All rights reserved.
Mami, What is Immigration?

Written by Anissa Pérez
Edited by Hector Perla and Alexander Barrientos
Illustrated and designed by Nicol Belvedere

979-8-9900339-2-4

This book is dedicated to

my son, Samito; my husband, Hector, an immigrant from Central America; and all of the immigrants who add indescribable beauty to this nation and world.

We see you. We hear you. We love you.

"Mami, I heard a friend mention the word, immigration, at school. What is immigration?"

What a great question, Sammy! Immigration is about people moving to a new country and staying there to live. They're called immigrants. Many immigrants leave what they love most in their home country to find a better life for themselves and their families. Many are looking for a better job or sometimes, a safer home.

It's not always easy for people to leave their home. They leave behind their:

- 🟩 Loved ones
- 🟦 Delicious food
- 🟥 Lifestyle
- 🟨 Community
- 🟧 Traditions
- 🟦 The sweet aroma of their home

They bring some of it to their new home, but it's never the same.
There's always a country-shaped hole in their heart.

Immigrants sometimes get mistreated when they arrive at their new home.

"Oh no, Mami, do they get sad?"

Many do since some people say mean things. Things like, "Go back to your country", and "We don't want you here." Those people may not understand or know immigrants. They may be afraid of them or may have bad feelings in their hearts toward them.

Can you imagine someone saying that to you?

"Mami, how can we welcome immigrants and be kind to our new neighbors in this country?"

Do the opposite of those who say mean things. Say kind things like, "Welcome to your new home. We're so happy to have you here. You can be your whole self in this country."

Here are other ideas:

Get to know them and their stories

Educate them about their rights

Speak for and stand up for their rights

Give them a warm plate of delicious food when needed most

Be their friend

Give clothing and shoes to those who may need it

 Ask if they need help finding a store that sells yummy food from their country

 Be a listening ear

 Invite them into your community and help them feel like they belong

 Be a shoulder to lean on

 Open your eyes to see their needs

 Have a heart to love them

And have a meal with them!

Now that you know what immigration is, share with your friends how to love and support our neighbors.

There are so many more incredible things about immigrants – and stories too. I cannot wait to share them with you!

One of Rev. Dr. Martin Luther King's quotes is always at the forefront of my mind —

> *I am convinced that men hate each other because they fear each other. They fear each other because they don't know each other, and they don't know each other because they don't communicate with each other, and they don't communicate with each other because they are separated from each other.*

I am raising a world changer, and this book is based on a real-life conversation I had with my then 4-year-old son. I did not want to keep this education and inspiration between us, but wanted to share it with anyone who would read it. I hope that you found it to be as inspiring!

We are not all immigrants, as this country once solely belonged to the Indigenous people, but most of us have come from somewhere else around the world in our family lineage — whether by choice or coercion.

There are so many other ways to honor and celebrate immigrants, and this book was merely a spark to get you and your children to light the fire to burn with passion to help immigrants arriving in your community.

Love immigrants.
Listen to them.
Get to know them.

I promise you will see the world in a whole new way — an extraordinarily beautiful way.

With love,
Anissa "Niss" Pérez

Daughter of an immigrant from El Salvador, spouse of an immigrant from El Salvador, and friend to many immigrants from around the world.

Book written on the ancestral land of the Piscataway people.

What are some other ideas to help immigrants?

1. _____
2. _____
3. _____
4. _____
5. _____
6. _____

www.ingramcontent.com/pod-product-compliance
Lightning Source LLC
LaVergne TN
LVRC080724070526
838199LV00041B/734